Martini-Henry .450 Rifles & Carbines

Dennis Lewis

Published by Excalibur Publications
PO Box 89667, Tucson, AZ 85752-9667
(520) 575-9057
excalibureditor@earthlink.net

ISBN # 1-880677-12-1   3P0804

Dedication

For my dad, Corral T. Lewis (1906-1986), who gave two sons his respect for and interest in firearms.

Contents

Introduction – Martini-Henry .450 Service Rifles

For the British Empire, the mid and late nineteenth century was a time of great power and responsibility. The Empire's vast colonial holdings, industrial enterprises and great wealth made it the leading world power.

However, this situation was not without its disadvantages. With the increased colonial holdings came increased military responsibilities throughout the world. From the frozen forests of Canada to the deserts of Egypt to the tropical rain forests of Africa, British troops were called on to face a variety of enemies. In addition Europe was becoming a less secure area as the nineteenth century progressed.

The period of relative peace that followed the defeat of Napoleon in 1815 was replaced by a growing number of conflicts on the continent. A resurgent France under the leadership of Napoleon III was countered by a newly-unified German Empire under the leadership of Bismarck. The Austro-Hungarian Empire and the Ottoman Empire faced increased political prob-lems within their own bound-aries, which weakened their influence in the rest of Europe. Russia, with problems at home, also was interested in expansion into areas of British control.

British military thinking had been greatly influenced by the many conflicts in the mid nineteenth century. The Crimean War (1854-1856), the American Civil War (1861-1865), and the Danish-Prussian War (1864) all helped convince the British of the need to modernize their military forces.

Paramount was the need to find a suitable breech loading rifle to replace the muzzleloading Pattern 1853 series of arms that then equipped the British military. The introduction of the Prussian needlefire breech loaders, the success of the various breechloading arms used in the American Civil war, and the adoption in 1866 of the Chassepot by France, convinced the British of the need to quickly find a breechloading rifle in order to maintain military parity with the other world powers.

As a stop gap measure the Snider system was introduced to convert many of the Pattern 1853 arms into breechloaders. When these arms ran out, new production Snider pattern arms were manufactured. From the start it was realized that the Snider was less then ideal as a military arm and the search for a new breechloading rifle was continued, though at a slower and more methodical pace.

An Ordnance Select Committee was formed in 1864 to begin the search for a service breechloader. Its first decision was the adoption of the Snider as mentioned above. But it also recommended that the search be continued for a more suitable pattern of arm. Through a series of exhaustive competitive trials, the Special Committee on Breech-loading Rifles decided to adopt the Martini-Henry Pattern Rifle as a service rifle in 1871. This rifle combined an action based on patents held by Friederich von Martini, and a rifling system developed by Alexander Henry.

The Martini-Henry series of arms in .450 caliber would re-

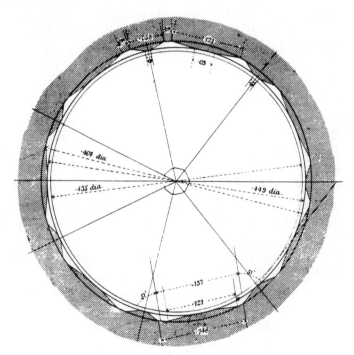

THE HENRY SYSTEM OF RIFLING,
Section showing bore enlarged 10 times.

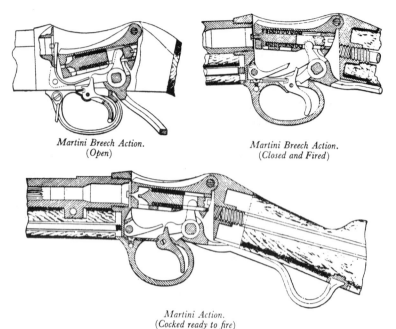

Martini Breech Action.
(Open)

Martini Breech Action.
(Closed and Fired)

Martini Action.
(Cocked ready to fire)
Fɪɢ. 2. *Martini action in three positions.*

main the standard arm for the British military until the advent of the Lee-Metford magazine rifles in the 1890s and for many colonial forces well into the twentieth century. Many of the .450 arms also were converted to .303 calibre and continued to soldier on with the British and colonial forces for an even longer period. Later, many of the Martini arms, both .450 and .303, were used as drill purpose arms. These can be found marked with "DP" stamped on both the wood and metal parts.

Commercial suppliers furnished many thousands of Martini-Henry arms to individual buyers, as well as for- eign governments. These arms are frequently of the same pattern as the standard British arms. However, others like the Swinburne carbines purchased by several colonial governments were of non standard pattern. The commercial suppliers also furnished many patterns of sporting arms on the Martini-Henry action and chambered for the .450 M-H cartridge.

Many of these Martini-Henry pattern arms have, over the years, been sold as surplus in some of the less-developed areas of the world. These arms, along with war reserve stocks and privately purchased arms, now form the bulk of the Martini-Henry type arms available to collectors.

Martini-Henry Mark I Rifle

The various versions of the Martini-Henry rifles served as the standard shoulder arm of the British Army's infantry and rifle regiments from the mid-1870s until the arms were replaced by the Lee-Metford rifle in the 1890s. The Martini-Henry rifles also were used by the Royal Navy and Royal Marines during this period. In addition, British militia and volunteer units were eventually equipped with the Martini-Henry rifles as production allowed.

Colonial governments acquired Martini-Henry rifles to arm their forces, and the Martini-Henry saw service in nearly every colony that the British had around the world. The Dominion of Canada, as well as the various Australian states, also armed parts of their forces with these rifles.

While all of the Martini-Henry rifles had similar characteristics, there were differences between the various production models. The following chapters will detail these differences.

After extensive testing of several different trials rifles the Mark I Martini-Henry rifle was approved for production

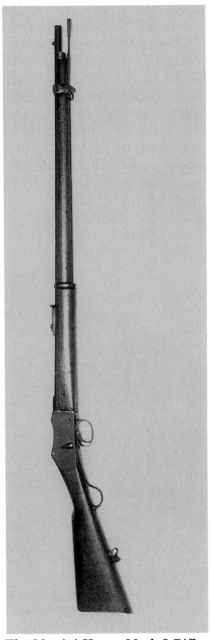

The Martini-Henry Mark I Rifle.

in 1871. Production of the rifle began at Royal Small Arms Factory (RSAF) Enfield. This new rifle proved to be less then satisfactory and underwent many changes between 1871 and 1876 when it was replaced by the Mark II pattern.

The Mark I rifle as originally introduced on June 3, 1871 closely resembled the last trials rifle. It consisted of a wooden buttstock with a checkered iron butt plate. This buttstock was available in a long and a short version to accommodate soldiers of different sizes.

The buttstock was bored from the rear to allow a stock bolt to pass through and screw into the rear of the receiver thus holding the stock firmly to the receiver. A small metal cup with a spring retainer in it was fitted to the bottom of the stock to retain the cocking lever in a closed position. A sling swivel was fitted to the rear of this.

The receiver consisted of a block of steel with the center milled out to hold the internal components. The rear of the receiver was shaped as a socket with a threaded hole to receive the thread of the stock bolt. The front of the receiver

Data stamped on the right side of this Martini-Henry Mark I receiver included the crown, V.R. (for Victoria, Regina), Enfield (the place of manufacture), 1873 (the date of manufacture), a view mark, and I (the model designation).

was drilled and threaded to receive the rear of the barrel and a recess was formed below that to receive the rear of the stock forend. Located in this recess was a hole that served to receive the rear of the cleaning rod.

A shallow checkered oval indentation was located on the right top rear of the receiver to serve as a thumb rest. Several holes were drilled through the side of the receiver to hold the various pins and screws used to hold the internal components. At the upper rear of the receiver a hole was bored through both sides to receive the pin around which the breechblock swiveled.

On the left side a smaller threaded hole was bored directly below this to hold a small screw that retained the breechblock pin. Another hole was bored at the bottom of the receiver that held a pin around which the cocking lever and tumbler rotated. The right side of this pin had a pointer formed on it that served as an indicator to show if the action was cocked or uncocked. This pin also retained the rear of the trigger plate and guard in the receiver.

Above this hole on the left side of the receiver was a small threaded hole for the keeper

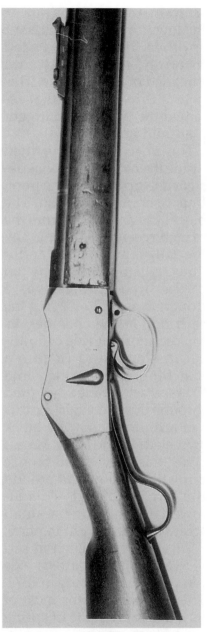

This view of the Mark I shows the overall arrangement of the cocking lever and indicator, the trigger guard assembly, the forend pinned to the action, and the rearsight.

screw that secured this pin. At the lower front of the receiver another hole was bored through the action and threaded on the left side. This held a threaded pin that retained the front of the trigger plate and guard.

The breech block was fitted inside the receiver and was designed to tip down at the front, thus opening the action. The block was drilled out from the rear to receive the firing pin, the coil mainspring, and a threaded stop nut. In the top of the breech block was a trough to assist in placing the cartridge in the chamber. Its top rear portion was cylindrical in shape and fit into a matching recess milled into the receiver. A hole was bored through this to contain the axis pin around which the block swiveled. In the early Mark I rifles, this was a solid bronze pin with a groove cut around the left hand end. This allowed the head of a small screw to lock the pin in place.

This screw loosened in service and a new pattern axis pin was fitted starting in 1874. This pin was slit for most of its length and made of spring steel. Flanges on either end fitted into recess milled around the axis pin hole.

A trigger plate and guard closed the bottom of the receiver. It contained several different parts all related to the firing mechanism. Along the right exterior of this plate was the safety, fitted only to the very earliest Mark I rifles. Very rarely found on surviving examples, it consisted of a checkered thumb piece visible at the right lower front of the receiver. This activated a locking bolt in the interior that prevented the trigger from being pulled.

The trigger was held in the plate by a screw and with the tumbler rest and tumbler formed the trigger group. The tumbler had an arm that engaged a slot in the firing pin and forced it back against the coil spring when the action was cocked. At the front of the trigger plate, the extractor was hinged around the front retaining pin. A hole was drilled through the upper front of the trigger bow and was used to retain the lower sling swivel.

The cocking lever was also hinged around the pin that retained the tumbler in the trigger plate. This lever had two arms that act on the breech-block to allow loading, and at the same time, cause the engagement of the tumbler, forcing the firing pin back and thus cocking the action when the lever was depressed. Depressing the lever also worked

Sections and Names of Components, "Martini" Breech Action

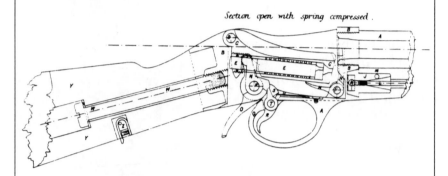

Section open with spring compressed.

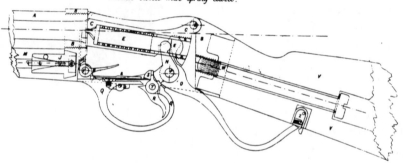

Section closed with spring eased.

AA	Barrel.	J	Rod & fore-end holder.	S	Tumbler rest.
BB	Body.	K	Rod & fore-end holder screw.	T	Trigger & rest axis-pin.
CC	Block.	L	Ramrod.	U	Trigger & rest spring.
D	Block axis pin *	M	Stock fore-end.	V	Stock butt.
E	Striker.	N	Tumbler.	W	Stock bolt.
F	Main spring.	O	Lever.	X	Stock bolt washer.
G	Stop nut.	P	Lever & tumbler axis-pin.	Z	Lever catch block spring & pin.
H	Extractor.	Q	Trigger plate & Guard.	a	Locking bolt.
I	Extractor axis-pin.	R	Trigger.	b	Thumbpiece.

The pin as shewn in this drawing is placed slightly too low.

These illustrations are from *Trajectory Etc. of the Martini-Henry Rifle*, published by the School of Musketry, Hythe, 1st February 1873.

the extractor, tipping it back and ejecting the cartridge.

The barrel was screwed into the receiver and was 33.22 inches in length from the chamber end of the barrel to the muzzle. Immediately in front of the threaded portion of the breech was the knoxform, a flat-topped, raised portion that butted up against the receiver. Below this was a lug with a hole drilled through it.

The rear sight was brazed and screwed to the barrel 6.25 inches from the receiver. This sight consisted of a base calibrated on the right side from 100 to 400 yards. Two raised ramps were located at the top with a flat leaf spring secured by a screw at the front located between them. The spring provided the tension necessary to retain the sight leaf in position. The sight leaf was hinged to the base at the rear and was graduated to 1,300 yards.

The front sight was located 1-5/16 inches from the muzzle, and took the form of a barleycorn set on a block. The front sight also served as a bayonet lug for the socket bayonet fitted to some Martini-Henry rifles.

The rifle's forend was secured to the barrel and receiver by two split bands and

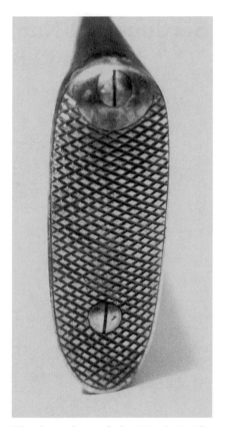

The buttplate of the Mark I rifle is distinctive in that it is fully chequered. Later versions of the Martini-Henry omitted this enhancement.

a pin. This pin passed through the block on the rear underside of the barrel. The upper band had a bayonet lug formed on its right hand side for the various sword bayonets used on the Martini-Henry rifles and also carried the upper sling swivel. It seated against a shoulder on the forend located 2.25 inches from the muzzle end of the stock. In addition to being held by the clamping action of the screw that held the sling swivel, it was secured by a plain pin that passed through the middle of the band and the stock.

The rear band was also a clamping band and seated against a shoulder located 18.25 inches from the muzzle end of the stock. To keep the band from moving forward under recoil a small diameter steel pin was inserted in the stock immediately in front of the band and left protruding on both sides of the forend. A steel cap was located at the muzzle end of the forend to protect the stock from splitting. It was held to the forend by a single screw that was lo-cated in the bottom of the barrel channel.

The forend also contained the channel for the cleaning rod. This channel was an open trough running from the muzzle to the rear band and then bored through the remainder of the forend coming out at the back to match the similar diameter hole bored in the front of the receiver.

A rod retainer consisting of a 2.5 inch long steel plate with a raised lip at the front end was located in the bottom of the ramrod channel immediately behind the nosecap. It was secured in place by two screws passing through the bottom of the barrel channel. The raised lip matched a notch cut in the cleaning rod to re-

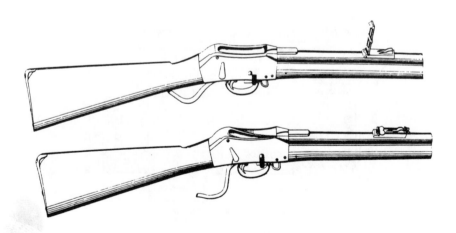

The top view of the Martini-Henry shows the action closed and the rearsight raised. The bottom view shows the action open and the rearsight in its folded position.

tain it in its channel.

The ramrod was 32.75 inches long and had a right hand thread at the lower end for attaching a cleaning jag. The upper end swelled out to form a square faced shoulder four inches from the knob-like end that had a hole bored through it. The square shoulder was designed to snap in place behind the rod retainer in the bottom of the cleaning rod channel. In order to remove the rod, it was necessary to spring the rod outward past the retainer and then pull the rod forward.

This was the Mark I Martini-Henry Rifle as originally adopted. After a brief time in the hands of troops in the field, this pattern was found to have several shortcomings. Problems with the trigger assembly, the striker, safety mechanism, breech block axis pin, cleaning rod, and sighting resulted in changes being made to the rifle.

A second pattern was sealed on September 3, 1872, and for the first time the rifle was referred to as the Mark I in official records. This had changes made to the trigger assembly in an effort to correct the problems reported from the field.

A third pattern of Mark I Martini-Henry Rifle was approved on July 17, 1874. This became the most widely produced and used version of the Mark I rifles. In place of the bronze breech block axis pin, a split steel pin was fitted. This

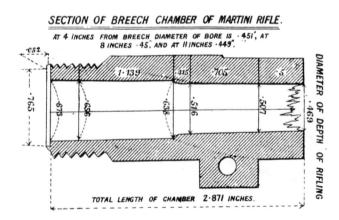

SECTION OF BREECH CHAMBER OF MARTINI RIFLE.

AT 4 INCHES FROM BREECH DIAMETER OF BORE IS ·451", AT 8 INCHES ·45". AND AT 11 INCHES ·449".

TOTAL LENGTH OF CHAMBER 2·871 INCHES.

This view of the breech area of the Martini-Henry is from *Trajectory Etc. of the Martini-Henry Rifle*, published by the School of Musketry, Hythe, 1st February 1873.

16

required that the axis pin retaining screw and its mounting hole be eliminated and that a recess for the end of the new pin be cut into the left side of the receiver.

On arms converted to this pattern the hole was filled in and a recess cut that allowed the new pin to be used. The cleaning rod had the swelled portion modified on one side to form a cam to make it possible to remove the rod without springing it. The safety catch was deleted as unnecessary. The trigger guard was modified by removing sharp edges, and a new longer buttstock was fitted along with a new smooth surfaced buttplate.

Early in 1875, the butt swivel was ordered deleted and to be removed from rifles in the field. A small wooden peg was used to fill in the hole. Rifles issued to rifle regiments continued to have the butt swivel fitted.

Perhaps the most important functional change came about as a result of the failure of large numbers of strikers during field trials. To alleviate this problem the striker was redesigned and strengthened. This also required changes to be made to the breech block to allow the new striker to be fitted. These changes took place during 1873-74. Modified blocks are marked "'74" on the side. The problem of broken firing pins was not fully solved until the introduction of the new breech block and firing pin fitted to the Martini-Henry cavalry carbine in 1877, and later to the Mark III rifle in 1879.

Mark I rifles may be encountered that do not precisely match the sealed patterns. Many rifles on issue to the colonies were not upgraded to third pattern status and may be found to retain the bronze axis pin or some earlier features. Many Mark I rifles were also later upgraded to Mark II status, but may or may not retain earlier features such as the checkered butt plate.

In addition to being manufactured at Royal Small Arms Factory at Enfield Lock (RSAF Enfield), the Mark I rifle was manufactured at Birmingham Small Arms Company (BSA) and London Small Arms Company (LSA).

The Martini-Henry Mark I rifle carried the Queen's crown, the initials "VR," place of manufacture, year of manufacture, small crown over broad arrow, and the roman numeral "I" on the right side of the receiver. The butt stock carried the manufacturer's roundel and roman numeral "I."

Martini-Henry Mark II Rifle

The Mark I rifle that had been approved on July 17, 1874 was still considered less than satisfactory, and was the subject of many proposed modifications. Problems were still being encountered with the trigger assembly, and the Royal Small Arms Factory (RSAF) at Enfield accommodated this problem by developing an improved trigger assembly.

This trigger assembly was to become part of the reason that the nomenclature was advanced to Mark II on April 25, 1877. In addition to the new trigger, the Mark II had the rear sight modified and the breech block modified.

The modified trigger assembly did away with the complicated tumbler rest assembly and substituted a tumbler that acted directly on the trigger, as well as a new pattern trigger. At the same time the trigger guard was redesigned to better exclude dirt from entering the action.

Experience in the field had shown that the rear sight notches were too fine for good sighting. The sights fitted to the Mark II had the notches deepened and the slide en-

The Martini-Henry Mark II Rifle.

larged to maintain the proper relationship with the front sight.

Modifications also were made to the breechblock. A slot was cut in the bottom of the breech block to provide clearance for the new tumbler when it was lowered for loading. The top of the breech block on the Mark I rifles had been polished bright. This had proven difficult to keep bright as a result of the corrosive effects of the blackpowder cartridges fired in it, much to the dislike of the soldiers who were required to keep it clean. To make this task easier the top of the block, was now to be "browned." Actually, the color was closer to the bluing found on most arms.

A new cleaning rod had been approved in 1876. This rod was of the same length and still had the threaded end for the jag, but had a redesigned upper end. The rod was now tulip headed with a oblong hole cut through it. Instead of having a swell ending in a sharp shoulder, the rod now had a swell with a slot cut in it to engage the rod retainer. One side was left uncut to act as a cam that made withdrawing the rod easier.

All other features of the Mark I were carried forward into the new rifle. It also was planned that all the Mark I rifles would be updated to this pattern and remarked as Mark II rifles. Such rifles can be identified by the pre-1877 date

The action of the Mark II rifle shows the standard Martini-Henry nomenclature: crown, V.R., BSA&M Co. (Birmingham Small Arms & Manufacturing Company, the manufacturer), 1889 (year of production), view mark, and II (model designation).

19

on the side of the receiver.

With the adoption of the improved Mark III in 1879 production of the Mark II rifle would have been expected to end. However, Birmingham Small Arms Company continued to produce the Mark II into 1890 for government contracts.

The Martini-Henry Mark II rifle was manufactured by not only RSAF Enfield and BSA, but also by London Small Arms Company (LSA) and National Arms and Ammunition Company (NAA).

The manufacturer's name will appear on the side of the receiver, along with the royal cypher, year of manufacture, a small crown over broad arrow, and the roman numeral "II." The buttstock was marked with the manufacturer's rondel and the roman numeral "II."

The muzzle section of the Mark II rifle shows the barleycorn foresight, cleaning rod, forend cap, front band with bayonet stud, and front sling swivel.

Martini-Henry Mark III Rifle

The Martini-Henry Mark III Rifle.

On August 22, 1879, a new pattern of Martini-Henry rifle was sealed for manufacture. The new rifle made use of improvements made in the production of the action as used on the Martini-Henry carbines and improvements suggested by reports from the field. While the outward appearance of most of the parts of the new Mark III rifle changed little from the earlier Mark I or Mark II rifles, significant changes were made in an effort to furnish a more robust arm for British forces.

Perhaps the most noticeable change occurred in the method of attachment for the forend. The forend was no longer attached by a pin passing through a block on the bottom of the barrel but rather by a hook arrangement that engaged the front of the receiver. This hook was in the form of a flat piece of steel inlet into the bottom rear of the forend and fastened to it by two wood screws. The front of this flat piece had a raised lip on the end that engaged a matching recess in the front lower side of the receiver. The front of the receiver was no longer formed as an open bot-

Information stamped on the right side of the Martini-Henry Mark III action follows the style of the earlier marks. This rifle was manufactured at the Royal Small Arms Factory at Enfield Lock.

tomed mortise, but instead had a closed bottom that contained this recess. The forend also was lengthened .312 inch.

A new breech block was introduced for use in cavalry carbines in 1877, and was also used in the new rifle. The new block was made wider to increase the steadiness of movement when the action was opened and closed. The diameter of the firing pin hole was also increased by .002-inch. The new breech block was to be used in all rifles and carbines produced after 1879. It could also be used to repair Mark II rifles if the Mark II

striker and retaining nut were fitted. The block is marked on the side with a "III."

The striker also was improved. The diameter of the point was decreased .002-inch to give it more clearance. The body of the striker was increased in diameter to make it stronger and to make it move in its recess easier. The slot for the tumbler was also reduced in width by .010-inch also to strengthen the striker. Dimensional changes were also made to the retainer nut.

The cocking indicator was of the same pattern as that used on the carbine which was smaller then that used on the Mark I and Mark II rifles. Again, this is a noticeable exterior change.

A change in the shape of the rear of the barrel also was made to make a better mating surface with the receiver. A lump was formed on the underside of the barrel, similar to that on the top. This provided an enlarged bearing surface when the barrel was screwed into the receiver, and strengthened the breech area of the barrel. Modifications to the forend inletting were made to accommodate this change.

Continued problems with the sights led to modifications to the rear sight. To correct the problem of deflection resulting from the rifling the rear sight was attached to the barrel slightly to the left of center. This gave the leaf a inclination of one degree and six minutes. The sight bed also was lengthened .125-inch to support the leaf and end cap better. It also was necessary to lengthen the rear sight spring the same amount.

Mark III rifles were manufactured at RSAF Enfield, Birmingham Small Arms Company (BSA), London Small Arms Company (LSA), National Arms and Ammunition Company (NAA), and Henry Rifled Barrel Company (HRB). Production continued into the 1890s, with the majority of those produced going to colo-

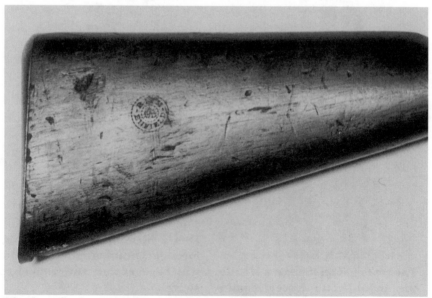

The buttstock of this Martini-Henry rifle clearly shows the place of manufacture — Enfield — stamped in the rondel.

nial forces, the militia, and volunteer units.

Martini-Henry Mark III rifles will be found marked on the receiver with the Queen's crown and "VR" forming the royal cypher, the name of the manufacturer, the crowned broad arrow, the roman numeral "III," and below that the Arabic numeral "1."

The buttstock was marked with the maker's rondel, a roman numeral "III," and the Arabic numeral "1."

The rearsight on the Mark III rifle was modified to correct continued problems which surfaced in earlier marks.

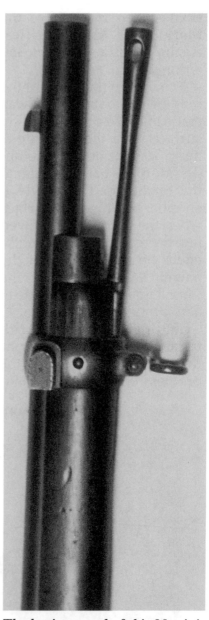

The business end of this Martini-Henry Mark III rifle shows the foresight, cleaning rod, front band with bayonet stud, and front sling swivel.

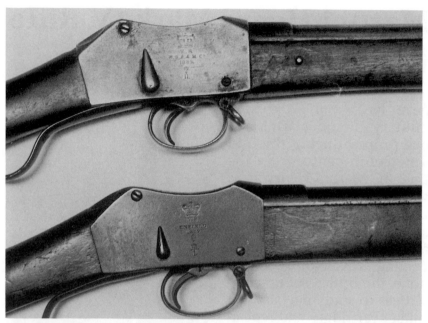

A comparison is shown between the Martini-Henry Mark II and Mark III rifles. In both upper and lower photos, the Mark II is at the top and the Mark III on the bottom. Note especially the different methods of attaching the forends.

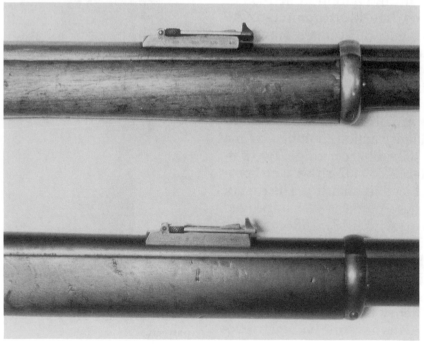

Martini-Henry Mark IV Rifle

The Martini-Henry Mark IV was the .450 rifle that should never have been. Progress in military shoulder arms had been rapid during the mid nineteenth century. By the time the Martini-Henry arms were in service with the British army, other nations were already moving towards adopting new small bore repeating arms. Not to be outdone, the British set up committees to study new smaller caliber cartridges and repeating arms.

The search for the new cartridge and rifle culminated with the adoption in 1888 of the Lee-Metford magazine rifle in .303 caliber. However, as a result of this search for a new cartridge and rifle another combination was also developed. This arm took the form of an improved Martini-Henry action chambered for a .402 caliber cartridge. Two patterns of .402 rifles were produced in quantity. The first of these patterns was approved on April 17, 1886, as the Enfield-Martini Rifle .4 inch. Field trials proved that this radical new design was not as serviceable as the Martini-Henry rifles then in service. This new rifle had such revo-

The Martini-Henry Mark IV rifle, A pattern.

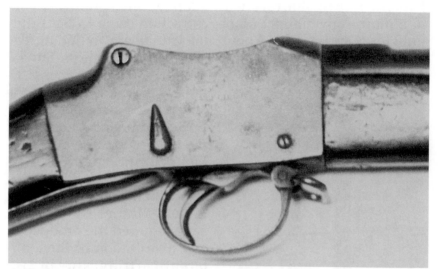

This A pattern action shows signs of considerable use in the defense of the British Empire.

lutionary features as a quick loader attached to the right side of the action, a safety, and a new form of stocking up. A new sword bayonet also was designed for the rifle.

A second pattern of Enfield-Martini was approved on May 13, 1887. Designated Enfield-Martini Rifle .4 inch Second

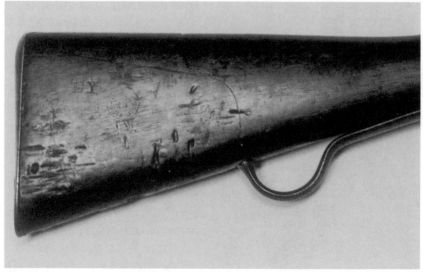

The A pattern buttstock shows evidence of hard use around the manufacturer's rondel and the model designation.

Pattern, the new rifle reverted to a more conventional Martini-Henry appearance. A new extended operating lever was

The Martini-Henry Mark IV rifle, B pattern.

adopted after problems with extraction came to light during campaigns in Sudan. The .4" cartridge with its Enfield designed 7-groove rachet rifling was retained as was the new pattern sword bayonet.

The imminent adoption of the .303" cartridge and Lee-Metford rifle, the .450" Martini-Henry rifles already in service, and the new .4 inch Enfield-Martini rifles would have required the production and distribution of three different cartridges to British forces. This was viewed with alarm by the supply services of the British military, yet large quantities of the new .4" rifles had been produced at Enfield during 1887 and 1888. These rifles represented a substantial investment, and it was hoped that they might be adopted to use the .450" cartridge and be issued to colonial, reserve, and volunteer forces.

On September 15, 1887, three separate patterns of Martini-Henry Mark IV rifles in .450" were approved for production. These rifles were designated Mark IV A, B, and C. Maximum use of Enfield-Martini components was made in producing the new rifles, and approximately 100,000 Mark IV rifles were produced.

The Mark IV's receiver was different from the earlier Mar-

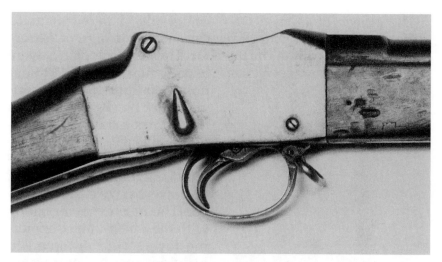

The B pattern action of the Martini-Henry Mark IV rifle.

tini-Henry arms. It retained the receiver designed for the Enfield-Martini Second Pattern rifle. When the conversions of the Enfield-Martini First Pattern rifles were made, the new Second Pattern receiver was used since the First Pattern receiver was different and unsuitable for conversion.

Externally, the most noticeable feature was the cut down rear portion of the receiver. Where the original Martini action sloped back to join the buttstock, the new action was stepped down immediately behind the breech block axis pin to form a more comfortable grip.

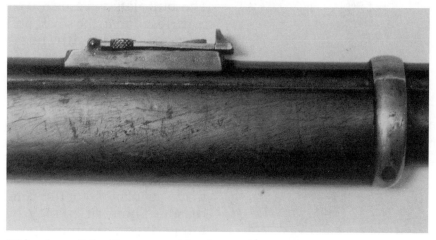

This view of the B pattern rifle shows the rearsight and middle band on the forend.

The breech block also was different. The body was narrowed and the angle on the underside changed so as to clear a new design of extractor. These breech blocks were usually marked "E-M" to denote their Enfield-Martini origin. Later blocks produced as new parts carry the roman numeral "IV"

The new extractor was .5-inch longer and had a slot in the lower arm to clear the trigger. The new extractor, along with the 3 inch-longer operating lever, were designed to provide positive extraction and correct the problems with the extraction of fired cases that had appeared during the Sudan Campaign.

The buttstock also was of different design from the earlier Martini-Henry rifles. It was narrowed in cross section, and the angle of the buttplate in relation to the bore was changed to improve sighting. The buttplate was narrowed to correspond to the stock, and was attached with brass screws to prevent the buttplate screws from rusting and freezing in place. A thin brass liner also was inserted between the buttplate and the stock to prevent corrosion. The cup that held the end of the operating lever also was made out of brass for the same reason. Some rifles may be found fitted with iron caps.

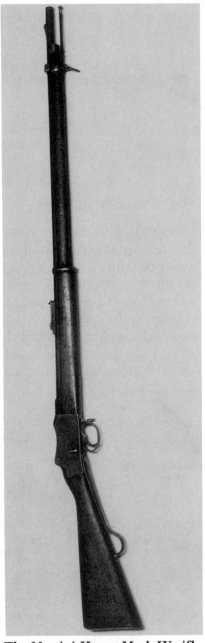

The Martini-Henry Mark IV rifle, C pattern.

Changes in the forend were

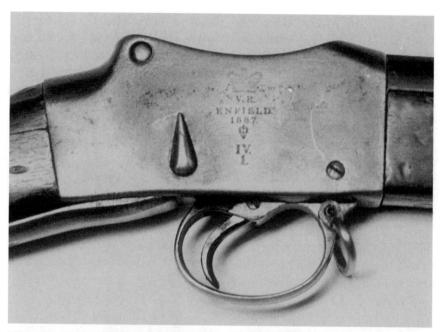

This Mark IV C pattern action shows that it was namufactured at the Royal Small Arms Factory at Enfield Lock in 1887.

relatively minor when compared with the Mark III rifle. A new nosecap was installed with the cleaning rod catch integral rather then separate, as it had been since the Mark I. The bands, swivels, and forend hooks were the same as

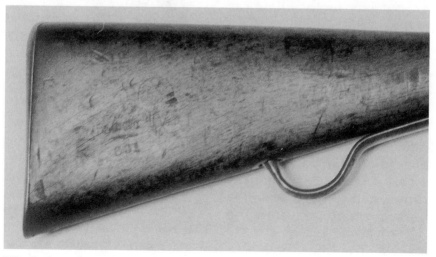

The buttstock on this C pattern rifle carries the Enfield-manufactured Mark IV rondel.

used on the Mark III rifle. They will be found to carry the "E-M" markings occasionally, or the more common "WD" or "III" markings of the earlier Martini-Henry rifles.

Cleaning rods for the Mark IV rifles were different from the earlier pattern of Martini-Henry rifles. The rod was originally designed for use with the Enfield-Martini rifle. The 32.75 inches long rod was threaded at its lower end to take a cleaning jag. The upper end was slightly swelled and had a cupped end with a slot directly below it. A swell was located below this with a groove completely cut around the rod 3-3/4 inches from the tip. The slot engaged the rod retainer on the nosecap. Like the Mark I rifle's first rod, it was necessary to spring the rod out in order to pull it clear of the forend.

Barrels on the Mark IV rifles were different among the three patterns. The A and B pattern rifles had barrels that were .125-inch shorter then the C pattern, and were fabricated from the original .4-inch Enfield-Martini barrels.

This necessitated reboring, rifling, and rechambering the barrel, which required the .125-inch shortening for the process. The Mark IV, A Pattern barrel will be found to have a very short knoxform with a filler block brazed to the top. This served to fill the space formerly occupied by the Enfield Martini, First Pattern rifle's short range rear sight.

The Mark IV, B Pattern bar-

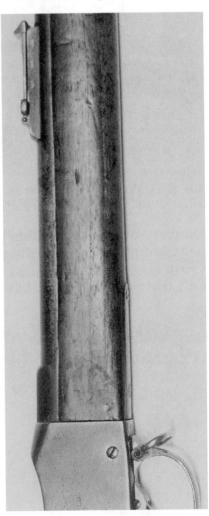

The rearsight on the Martini-Henry Mark IV, C pattern was the same sight as used on the Mark III rifle.

rel had the knoxform shortened .125-inch in the reboring process, but otherwise did not require any further modification.

Mark IV, C Pattern barrels were identical to the Mark III Martini-Henry barrel in length.

Sighting of the Mark IV rifle was the same as for the Mark III rifle. However, two forms of front sight were used. The A Pattern rifles used a block with the barleycorn set on it, like the earlier Martini-Henry rifles.

The B and C Pattern rifles had the barleycorn set on a block with an inclined ramp running to the rear. This was the pattern front sight that had been fitted to the Enfield-Martini Second Pattern rifles. Only the A Pattern could fit a socket bayonet. The B and C Patterns with the inclined ramp could only be fitted with sword pattern bayonets.

While the A and B Pattern rifles were conversions, the C Pattern rifles were built using either a mix of Enfield-Martini parts and new parts or all new parts. As the Mark IV rifles remained in service in the colonial forces and the Indian Army for many years, repairs have further aggravated this mix of parts.

All Martini-Henry Mark IV

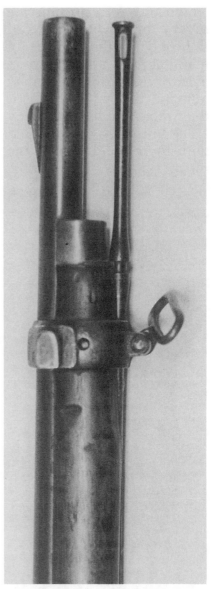

The foresight on the C pattern Mark IV rifle was considerably different from that on the A pattern.

rifles were manufactured at RSAF Enfield. Receivers were marked with the Queen's crown and "VR" forming the royal cypher, with the word Enfield below that, the year of manufacture, a small crown over a broad arrow, the roman numeral "IV," and below that the Arabic number "1."

The buttstock was marked with the Enfield rondel, the roman numeral "IV," and the Arabic numeral "1" on the right side at the rear. Additional markings may be found on the buttstock indicating issue to various units and overhauls at ordnance depots.

Large numbers of Mark IV rifles were issued to Indian army units and carry Indian markings.

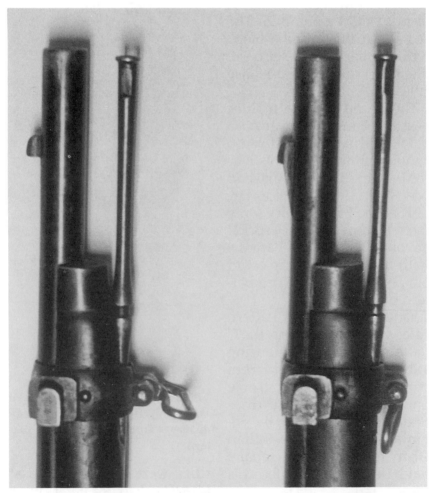

A comparison between the Martini-Henry Mark IV, A pattern (left), and B pattern (right), shows a difference in foresight styles.

34

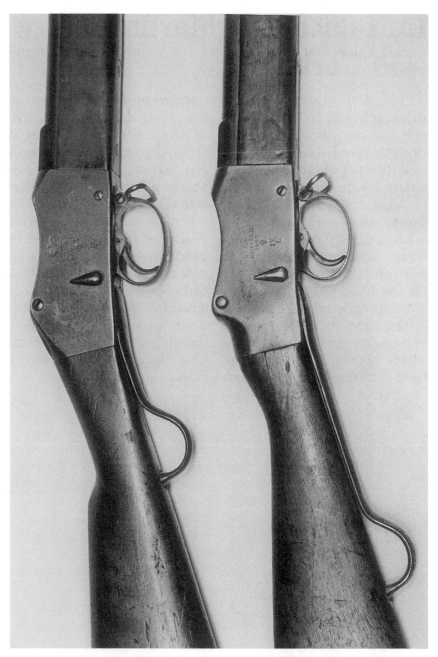

The Martini-Henry Mark IV, C pattern (right) shows a number of differences when compared with the Martini-Henry Mark III rifle, (left). Note especially the shape of the action, as well as the lengths of the two cocking levers.

Introduction – Martini-Henry .450 Carbines

The .450 Martini-Henry rifles proved to be satisfactory arms for the infantry and rifle units of the British and colonial forces, but were not considered suitable for issue to cavalry and artillery units. These units were equipped with specially designed carbines based on the Snider action, and new patterns based on the Martini-Henry action were considered desirable.

Development of the carbine versions of the Martini-Henry series occurred at the same time as that of the rifles. As an improvement was made in either the rifle or carbine, that improvement was normally applied to the other version. No carbine versions of the Martini-Henry Mark IV were introduced.

Versions of the carbine were produced for issue to cavalry, garrison artillery, field artillery, and horse artillery. These carbines were also issued to colonial, militia, volunteer units, police, and later used widely as drill purpose arms like the various patterns of rifles.

Martini-Henry Carbine Mark I

A carbine version of the Martini-Henry was approved for service on December 1, 1877. This carbine was intended to be suitable for use by the cavalry, garrison artillery, horse artillery, and field artillery. It would, in fact, replace the cavalry and artillery carbine patterns of the Snider system with one arm. Soon after the introduction of the Mark I carbine, it was realized that one pattern would not serve to meet the needs of both the cavalry and artillery.

After prolonged development problems, primarily relating to excessive recoil of the rifle cartridge in the much lighter carbine, a new reduced load cartridge was introduced. This cartridge used a 410-grain bullet with 70 grains of black powder, instead of the more potent rifle loading of a 480-grain bullet with 85 grains of powder. Trials showed this cartridge to be pleasant to shoot, and in an emergency either the carbine or rifle cartridge could be used in either arm.

This new carbine resembled the rifle in many ways. The buttstock was almost identical to the rifle. the only difference

Martini-Henry Carbine Mark I.

This Mark I Carbine gives evidence as to its lineage on the right side of the receiver: the crown, VR, Enfield, 1879, view mark, and model designation.

being the deletion of the lower sling swivel.

The carbine action differed from the Martini-Henry Mark II rifle action only in minor ways. The receiver body was rounded off at the lower forward corners to improve entry into the saddle buckets used by the cavalry. The head of the cocking indicator was also reduced in size, and this is quite noticeable when compared with that on the rifle.

Internally the breech block differed from that of the Mark II rifle. It was made wider at the front to steady its movement in the receiver and was fitted with a new striker assembly. The extractor also differs from the Mark II. The cutouts needed to clear the safety

that had been fitted to the earliest Martini-Henry Mark I rifles were dispensed with and the lower arm was now solid. In 1885 a new stronger extractor was developed and may be found fitted to earlier carbines and rifles. Such arms are marked "S X" on the receiver ring.

The forend of the carbine was attached to the receiver by a hook arrangement that engages a recess in the lower front of the receiver, rather then the stud and pin arrangement of the rifle. This hook took the form of a flat steel strap inlet into the bottom rear of the forend and held there by two wood screws. At its rear was a raised lip that hooked into the receiver's recess.

Barrels of the carbine also differed from the rifle. Not only were they shorter at 21.375 inches, but the breech form was changed. The knoxform had a matching projection on the bottom of the barrel, which made a stronger breech assembly.

The sights also were a different pattern. The front sight was a finer barleycorn, and had wings added on both sides to protect it from wear when being put in the saddle bucket.

The rear sight was sighted to 1,180 yards over the top of the leaf cap, and up to 1,000 yards on the leaf itself. The sight bed, marked from 100 to 400 yards, was attached to the barrel by a dovetail at the front and a screw at the rear, instead of being soldered to the barrel as was done on the rifle.

Two bands secured the forend to the barrel. The rear one was located about halfway back from the muzzle. It was split at the bottom and secured with a screw that applied a clamping action to it. The upper band was wider and solid, secured by a pin that passed through it and the nosecap.

At the front of the forend was a nosecap, held by two screws that passed through the forend from the inside of

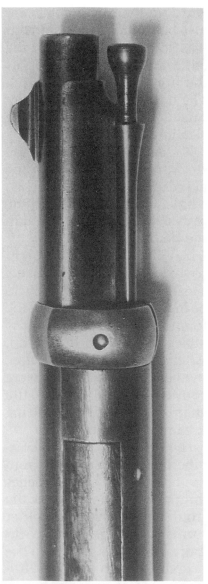

The muzzle of the Mark I Carbine shows the distinctive foresight, the cleaning rod, and the front band.

the barrel channel on each side of the cleaning rod channel. The nosecap extended forward on the barrel to a point just below the front sight. It was scalloped in front of the band and served to support the front of the cleaning rod. The nosecap also contained a raised lip that retained the cleaning rod.

A channel was cut into the stock, running back from the nosecap to the rear band. Then a hole was bored through the rest of the forend to contain the cleaning rod.

In 1879, a leather rear sight cover was approved for issue. This required a wood screw to be installed on each side of the forend below the rear sight to attach the cover to the forend. After the initial introduction, the heads of the screws were rounded off to reduce the chance of snagging or cutting the uniforms of the users.

The cleaning rod for the carbine differed in design from the rifle rod. It was 21 inches long and swelled out at the front with a sharp shoulder formed near the front to engage the rod catch on the nosecap. It then extended forward a short distance before ending in a bulbous tip. The lower end was threaded to fit a cleaning jag.

This then was the Carbine, Martini-Henry, Mark I as originally produced for use by cavalry and artillery units.

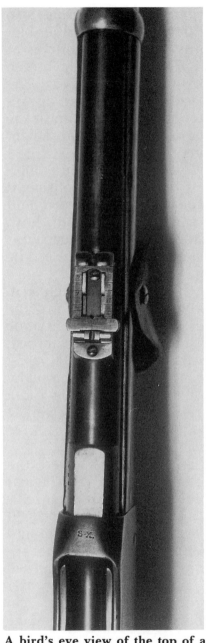

A bird's eye view of the top of a Martini-Henry Carbine Mark I shows the forward portion of the breechblock, the knoxform, the rearight (with leather cover fastened below), and middle band.

40

Changes to this carbine were made from time to time as improvements were developed or needs changed. These included the fixing of a leather cover for the rear sight, as previously noted, the modification of the forend hook, and the addition of a sling swivel to the heel of the buttstock. This last modification was to allow the use of a sling with the carbine. The sling attached to the upper end of the carbine with a leather loop.

Mark I carbines may be found with other modifications, such as the addition of a sling swivel to the upper band, allowing the use of a normal style sling.

Martini-Henry Garrison Artillery Carbine

Shortly after the introduction of the Mark I carbine it was decided that it would not serve the needs of the garrison artillery and modifications to the existing carbine were proposed. The Army felt that the garrison artillery required a carbine that would fix a bayonet. As produced, the Mark I Carbine could not fix a bayonet.

Ultimately, the decision was taken to modify the Mark I carbine to fix a sword bayonet. The bayonet itself was to be modified from the Yataghan bayonet used on the Snider artillery carbines. The only change needed was the bushing of the muzzle ring of the bayonet to accommodate the smaller diameter Martini-Henry barrel.

This bayonet was to be fixed only in emergencies, since it was felt that the combination was too short to be of much real use. When the Garrison Artillery Carbine was issued in 1878, it was done without the bayonets since a new bayonet was under development for use on the Martini-Henry artillery carbines.

To fit the bayonet, the following modifications were required. A new nose band with a bayonet lug on its right side was fitted, similar to the one found on the Martini-Henry rifles. The length of the bayonet's hilt required that this band also be moved fur-

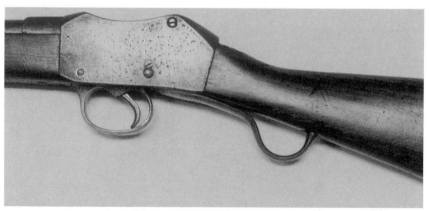

This Garrison Artillery Carbine shows evidence of hard use, as can be seen by the amount of wear on the action of the arm.

ther from the muzzle so that the bayonet's muzzle ring could fit over the carbine's muzzle. Modifications to the cleaning rod also were required.

The rod on the original Mark I carbine extended to a point even with the muzzle of the gun. In order for the bayonet to be fitted, the rod had to be shortened to provide the required clearance for the bayonet cross guard. The shape of the end of the cleaning rod was changed at the same time, and took the form of a sphere rather then the tulip shaped tip used on the Mark I Carbine.

Martini-Henry Artillery Carbine Mark I

While the Garrison Artillery Carbine was being developed, the British government decided that all of the artillery units — garrison, field, and horse, should have a carbine that fixed a bayonet. While the garrison artillery did not require a sling, it was decided that the field and horse artillery did require one. This new pattern of carbine was approved for production in April of 1878.

The new carbine was fitted with sling swivels. One was located on the heel of the buttstock, 2-1/4 inches from the toe, while the other was located on the bottom of the upper band.

The upper band also carried the bayonet lug on its right side like the Garrison Artillery Carbine. But the lug had its front edge rounded off, to prevent injury to the user's hand.

Cleaning rods for the new Artillery Carbine were similar in length to the Garrison Artillery Carbine rod, but had a tulip-shaped head with a recess in its front surface. This recess was designed to clear the firing pin tip if the rod was dropped down the bore with the gun in an uncocked state.

The nomenclature of all carbines was changed as a result of the development of the Mark I Artillery Carbine. It was decided that the word

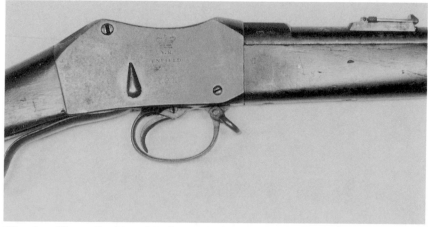

The Artrillery Carbine Mark I was developed to provide all artillery units with a carbine that fixed a bayonet.

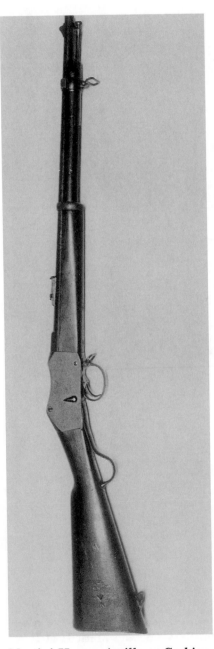

Martini-Henry Artillery Carbine Mark I.

"Garrison" would be discontinued, since all artillery units were to be equipped with the new carbine. In addition, the original Mark I Carbine for all services was to be known as the Martini-Henry Carbine Cavalry Mark I. These changes took place in 1879.

Bayonets for the new carbine were the subject of much debate. Eventually two patterns were accepted into service. These were the modified Pattern 1860 sword bayonet with bushed muzzle ring (similar to the pattern originally adopted for the Garrison Artillery Carbine), and the Artillery Carbine Bayonet Mark I or Pattern 1879 sword bayonet.

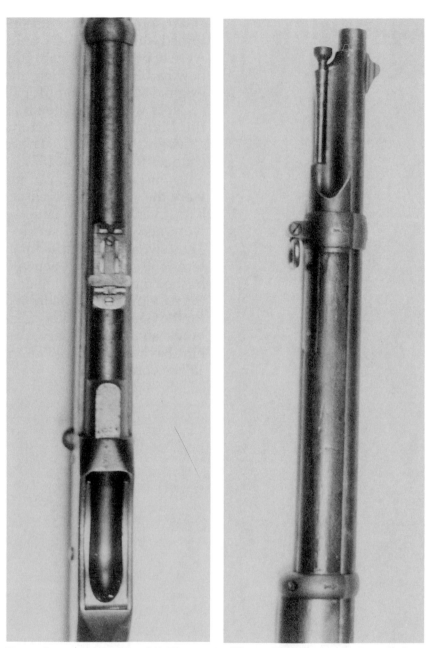

Two views of the Martini-Henry Artillery Carbine Mark I: at left, a view from above of the breechblock, rearsight and barrel; at right, the forend, bands, cleaning rod, foresight and muzzle.

Martini-Henry Artillery Carbine Mark II

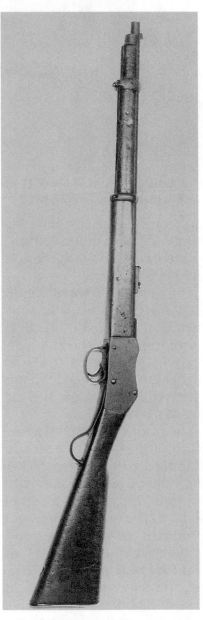

With the adoption of the .303 Cartridge and the Lee-Metford series of arms in 1888, the days of the .450 Martini-Henry should have been numbered. In an effort to save money and equip as many of the British forces with the new .303 arms the decision was taken to convert .450 Martini arms into .303 rifles and carbines suitable for issue to units not requiring the new magazine arms.

Large quantities of .450 arms and ammunition still remained in British stores. By the 1890s, the newer models of Martini-Henry arms were being converted to .303. This left a need for arms to fill the gap left by their withdrawal from service.

To fill this need, it was decided to take Martini-Henry Mark II rifles and convert them to a new pattern of artillery carbine. This arm was known as the Martini-Henry Artillery Carbine Mark II. It was approved on August 18, 1891 for use by Volunteer Artillery units and Colonial forces. The use of the Mark II rifle to produce this carbine resulted in their classification

Martini-Henry Artillery Carbine Mark II.

47

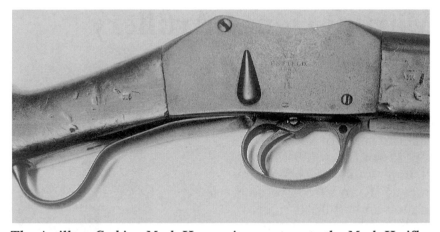

The Artillery Carbine Mark II owes it parentage to the Mark II rifle, from which it was converted.

as second class arms, since the Mark IIs had been downgraded with the adoption of the Mark III arms.

The conversion was straightforward, but at the same time provided a serviceable arm at minimum cost. The rifle barrel was shortened to 21.35 inches, and the muzzle diameter reduced to allow the fixing of a bayonet.

The front sight was attached to the muzzle and was of a standard rifle pattern rather than the carbine version with side wings. To protect the front sight, a special brass fore sight protector was designed and issued. A carbine pattern rear sight was soldered to the barrel, and the original rifle sight mounting holes were filled.

The rifle forend was shortened and the retaining shoulders for the bands moved to the rear. The hole for the rear band retaining pin was filled and new holes drilled for retaining pins for both bands. The nosecap was also refitted. The new forend was designed to come within 1 inch of the muzzle.

Modifications to the bands also were required. Both had the inside diameter expanded to accept the larger diameter of the barrel at their new locations. The upper band retained the sling swivel originally fitted when the arm was a rifle.

A marking disk was fitted to the buttstock to allow unit identifications to be placed on the carbine. A lower sling swivel was fitted to the lower rear of the buttstock to allow the fitting of a sling. All markings pertaining to the original Mark II rifle configuration were removed from the right side of the butt stock, and new markings were stamped in their place.

The receiver also was modified by fitting the Mark III extractor. This can be identified by the "S-X" stamped into the top of the receiver ring or by disassembling the action. The right side of the receiver retained the original rifle markings, while the new designation "MH .45" over "AC II" was stamped on the left side of the receiver. Not all Mark II Artillery Carbines seem to have been marked, and specimens may be found without these markings.

A new cleaning rod was designed for the Mark II Artillery Carbine. It is similar to the Mark II rifle rod, but shorter. No slot is cut in its head and the retaining groove is part of the swelled head rather then being located on a swell to the rear of the head. The lower end of the rod is threaded to accept a jag.

Production of these arms continued into the late 1890s. After their service with the Volunteer Artillery and other units many of the Mark II carbines were passed on to cadet corps along with other obsolete arms. At this time they were frequently marked with a "DP" on the butt stock and

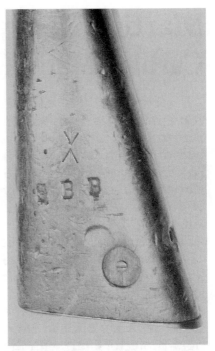

The buttstock on this Artillery Carbine Mark II shows the British government's sale mark — the two opposed broad arrows.

on the knoxform of the barrel. In addition a steel marking disk is usually fitted in place of the brass marking disk.

The bayonet used on the Mark II Artillery Carbine was the Pattern 1860 Sword Bayonet that had been used on the Enfield muzzleloading short rifles and the later Snider conversion short rifles, and later modified for the Mark I and other Martini-Henry rifles. This modification consisted of bushing the muzzle ring for the smaller diameter barrel of the .450 rifles.

Martini-Henry Artillery Carbine Mark III

A second artillery carbine conversion was adopted on September 2, 1891. This carbine differed from the Mark II Artillery Carbine in several features, although externally both carbines look quite similar.

This carbine used the action of the Martini-Henry Carbine Mark I with its rounded off lower front corners. It also employed the lighter carbine barrel with the built in front sight protectors, but with the same rear sight as fitted to the Mark II Artillery Carbine.

Unlike the Mark II pattern carbines the Mark III used a modified Mark III rifle forend. This was necessary because of the use of the later carbine or Mark III rifle style of receiver that featured a hook retained forend.

Modifications were similar to those used on the Mark II rifle forend for the Mark II Artillery Carbine. These included repositioning the bands and refitting the nosecap. The distance from the muzzle to the forend nosecap was two inches instead of one inch as on the Mark II Artillery Carbine.

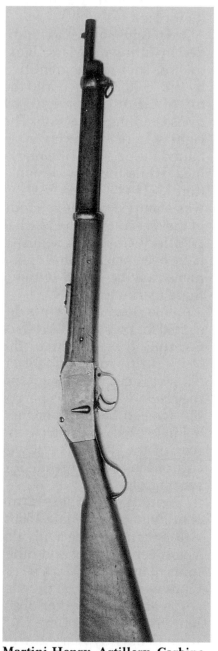

Martini-Henry Artillery Carbine Mark III.

This difference in forends resulted in the need for a different cleaning rod. While both rods were 21 inches in length, the shorter forend of the Mark III Artillery Carbine resulted in the locking groove for the cleaning rod being placed one inch further to the rear.

Production of the Mark III Artillery Carbine appears to have been very limited. Possibly only prototypes were assembled to guide conversion of Mark III rifle type actions into artillery carbines if needed.

Bayonets for the Mark III Artillery Carbine would have been similar to those produced for the Mark I Artillery Carbine.

Bands were repositioned and the nosecap refitted on the Artillery Carbine Mark III, at left.

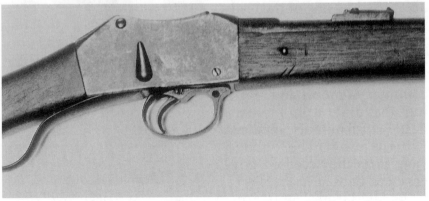

The Artillery Carbine Mark III used a modified rifle forend, in place of the traditional carbine forend wood.

Commercial .450 Martini-Henry Arms

Before the mass production of the Martini-Henry Mark I Rifle began, various commercial manufacturers were busy turning out commercial versions of the Martini-Henry for sales to civilians and foreign governments. The introduction of a new military arm was usually greeted in the United Kingdom with the development of civilian versions of the new arm for a variety of markets.

The Martini-Henry series was no different. Demand for the arms came from the Volunteer Corps, target shooters, officers, persons traveling overseas, Colonial governments, and various foreign governments interested in having the latest in military arms used by one of the leading world powers.

As a result many Martini-Henry arms, both rifles and carbines, will be found with commercial proofs and markings that differ from the standard British military versions. Patterns also will be found to vary from the accepted government guns.

Not all Martini-Henry arms were made by British manu-

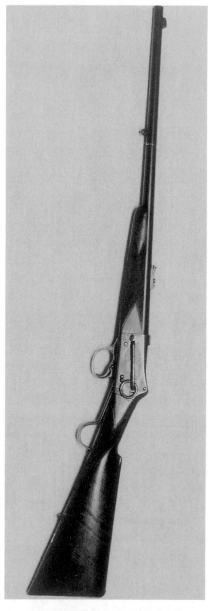

A commercial .450 Martini-Henry by T.W. Watson of London.

52

The right side of this T.W. Watson commercial .450 Martini-Henry rifle illustrates the fine engraving that could be found on such arms in the late nineteenth century.

facturers. A large number of Martini pattern arms were manufactured by the Providence Tool Company, Providence, Rhode Island, USA, for the Turkish Government and other foreign customers.

In addition, Providence Tool Company also manufactured sporting and target rifles based upon the Martini action for civilian sales. Many of Providence Tool Company' arms were not chambered for the .450 Martini-Henry cartridge.

British manufacturers and retailers provided the largest number of Martini-Henry commercial arms. Some of these arms were no more then government pattern arms with commercial markings,

while others represented the best work of the most prestigious gunmakers. Sporting and target arms by Westley Richards, Thomas Watson, W. J. Jeffrey & Co., R. B. Rodda, S. W. Silver & Co., W. W. Greener, C. G. Bonehill, Midland Gun Co., and others have been noted.

Perhaps the largest suppliers to the trade were the Birmingham Small Arms Company and the London Small Arms Company. Both of these arms makers supplied government pattern arms, as well as arms built to their own patterns. Many of these will be found marked with the names of retailers such as Alex. Fraser, Barnett, Henry Alport, Hollis, and the Army and Navy Co-

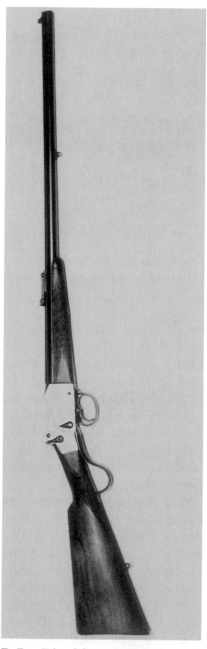

operative Society, in addition to or in place of the actual maker.

Some of the most interesting of these arms are the sporting arms based upon the Martini-Henry. These were frequently well engraved with fine quality French walnut stocks and with the finest checkering. Many of them were half stocked in either rifle or carbine lengths. Some had ribs added under the barrel to carry a cleaning rod, or over the barrel for a sighting rib. Many were fitted with express sights.

Most of these commercial arms were chambered for the .450 cartridge used by the British government. The advantage of having a rifle chambered for the standard government cartridge was not lost on officers and civilians buying a rifle to take overseas for hunting or protection.

The ability to obtain a proprietary cartridge could be very limited outside the United Kingdom. Of course, this did not mean that some of the commercial arms were not chambered for other cartridges, and such examples still can be found.

R.B. Rhodda of London & Calcutta is engraved on the barrel of this commercial .450 commercial Martini-Henry.

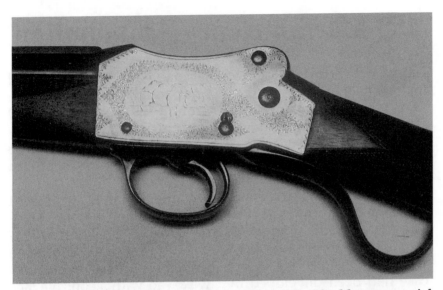

The left and right sides of the action of this R.B. Rhodda commercial .450 Martini-Henry sporting rifle are engraved with a rhinoceros and a tiger, perhaps an indication of the type of game for which the rifle was made.

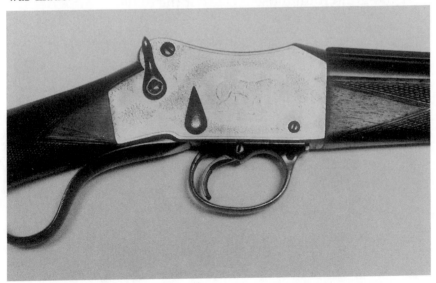

.450 Martini-Henry Ammunition

. The .450 cartridge adopted for use in the Martini-Henry arms was of a bottleneck design. Like the cartridge developed for the Snider arms, it made use of a case formed from sheet brass that was rolled around a former and attached to an iron base that also contained the primer. The interior of the case was lined with tissue paper. This type of case had been developed by Col. E. M. Boxer and had proved relatively trouble free when used in the Snider.

A 480-grain roundnose bullet made of 12 parts lead and one part tin with a paper patch around the base was loaded into this cartridge. It was secured by crimping the case into two cannelures located at the rear of the bullet.

A charge of 85 grains of black powder was the standard load. On top of the powder charge was placed a glazed card board disc, a beeswax wad with a concave face towards the bullet and two more glazed cardboard discs were located immediately under the bullet.

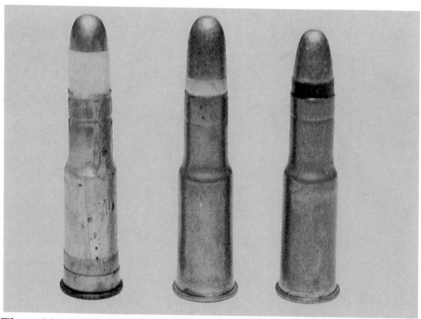

Three Martini-Henry cartridges: from left, a rolled case, solid case (both for the rifle), and a solid case carbine round.

This cartridge was adopted on August 16, 1873, as the Mark III and was produced with several minor variations.

On June 9, 1885, a solid brass .450 cartridge case was adopted for use in the Martini-Henry. This drawn brass case was a reaction to extraction problems experienced in Egypt and other theaters of operation. A change in the wad column also was made. This now consisted a wad of cotton fiber on top of the powder, a larger beeswax wad, and one glazed cardboard disc.

The bullet was still a 480-grain roundnose bullet with a paper patch. Unlike the earlier rounds it had only one cannelure.

A Mark II solid drawn case version was adopted on September 25, 1885. This version had a paper liner in the cartridge case and no cotton fiber wad was used. The wad column was now composed of one glazed cardboard disc, a beeswax wad, and two glazed cardboard discs.

Cartridges for the carbine versions of the Martini-Henry were similar in design. As mentioned in the section on carbines the rifle cartridge was found to be unpleasant to fire from the lighter carbines. This required a redesigned cartridge for use in the carbines.

It should be noted that in an emergency, ammunition for the rifle could be used in the carbine and carbine ammunition could be shot in the rifle. The first version of special carbine ammunition was adopted in 1877.

The major differences between the rifle and the carbine rounds was the weight of the bullet and the weight of the powder charge. The bullet was shortened .12 inches, thus reducing the weight by 70 grains to 410 grains. A corresponding reduction in the powder charge from 85 grains to 70 grains of black powder also was made. To take up the space caused by the reduction in powder volume, a wad of cotton fiber was placed on top of the powder. In the Mark II version this cotton fiber wad was eliminated. Other minor changes were made over the years.

A solid drawn case was adopted for use in the carbine on December 18, 1886. It was basically the Mark II Rifle cartridge case loaded with 63 to 67 grains of black powder and the 410-grain carbine bullet.

Other types of ammunition also were loaded for use in the Martini-Henry arms. On November 3, 1885, a buckshot cartridge containing 11 .275 inch diameter lead balls was

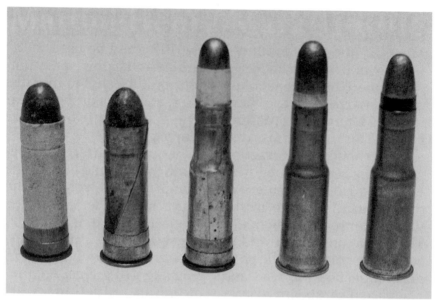

A comparison of Martini-Henry cartridges with those for the Snider-Enfield rifle. From left, Snider paper-covered round, Snider rolled case, Martini-Henry rolled case, Martini-Henry solid case, and Martini-Henry Carbine solid case.

introduced into service. Blanks were also manufactured for use in training exercises. These could be used in either the Martini-Henry or the Snider, thus reducing the number of types of ammunition required for use by British forces.

By the 1890s, versions of the .450 cartridge were being loaded with cordite instead of blackpowder. Much of this ammunition was for use in machine guns chambered for the .450. However, as time passed, cordite became the powder of choice, and even blanks were loaded with the new powder.

Bayonets

This brief overview of the various bayonets used with Martini-Henry rifles and carbines includes only the more common bayonets. Others produced for commercial sale, modified for cadet use, prototypes, and those produced for foreign contracts are not included.

Socket Bayonets

Pattern 1853, Bushed Socket

This is simply the standard Pattern 1853 Socket Bayonet as used on the Pattern 1853 Long Rifle, and the various models of Snider Long Rifles. To fit it to the smaller diameter Martini-Henry barrel, it was necessary to braze a bushing into the socket. The bayonet was carried in a leather scabbard with brass fittings. Several different patterns of this bayonet scabbard may be found.

Length overall: 20.7 inches
Blade length: 17 inches
Socket length: 3 inches

Pattern 1876, Socket Bayonet

The overall length of the Martini-Henry rifle and bayonet was considered by some to be too short for effective campaign use. To compensate for this, the chance to redesign the bayonet was taken when stocks of the Pattern 1853 bayonets began to run low.

The new bayonet was longer, had a new socket, and the blade design was changed. The blade was now equiangular in cross section, rather than having a wider top flat.

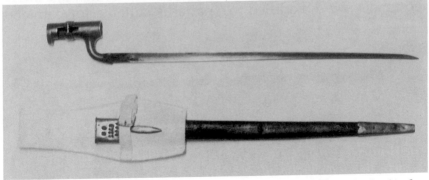

This early Martini-Henry socket bayonet is complete with the leather scabbard and frog.

Scabbards were produced in two patterns, and were brass mounted. These can easily be identified by, on the Mark I, having two rivets visible on the front face of the leather body; and on the Mark II version, having three rivets. These rivets secured a long leaf spring that helped retain the bayonet in the scabbard.

Length overall: 25.00 inches
Blade length: 21.75 inches

Sword Bayonets

Pattern 1856/58, Pattern 1858, Pattern 1860 Yataghan Sword Bayonet, Bushed for Martini-Henry

Just as the Pattern 1853 Socket Bayonet was adopted for the Martini-Henry rifles, the sword bayonets used with the various muzzleloading Enfield Short rifles and Snider Short rifles were modified to fit the Martini-Henry rifle.

This was accomplished by bushing the muzzle ring to the smaller diameter of the Martini-Henry rifle's muzzle, and where needed, making other changes in dimensions in the vicinity of the mortise slot at the back of the bayonet's hilt. This left a distinctive flat at that point. Scabbards for these bayonets were the same as used with the earlier rifles, and are steel mounted.

Length overall: 28.18 inches
Blade length: 22.75 inches

Cutlass Bayonets

Pattern 1871 Cutlass Bayonet

The Royal Navy had a requirement for a cutlass-type bayonet for issue with its Martini-Henry rifles. Production of new bayonets was contemplated, but quantities of earlier patterns suitable for conver-

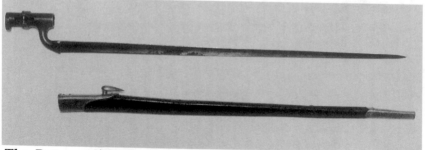

The Pattern 1876 Martini-Henry socket bayonet shows a different profile to the blade from the earlier Pattern 1853 style.

sion were available.

The conversion consisted of shortening and straightening the blade, and altering the form of the cup-shaped guard to a lighter pattern with a new cross piece containing the smaller diameter muzzle ring. The iron mounted scabbard also was modified.

Length overall: 31.3 inches
Blade length:　25.6 inches

Pattern 1859 Cutlass Bayonet, Bushed for Martini-Henry

This is the Pattern 1859 Cutlass Bayonet as used with the Snider Naval Rifle. The muzzle ring was bushed to enable its use on the Martini-Henry.

Length overall: 32.5 inches
Blade length:　26.8 inches

Artillery Sword Bayonets

Pattern 1879 Artillery Bayonet, Converted

These bayonets were produced from Pattern 1859 Cutlass Bayonets. The conversion involved modifications to the guard, muzzle ring, and blade. Perhaps the most noticeable feature was the provision of a 9.25 inch saw on the upper side of the blade.

The iron mounted scabbard was also modified. These bayonets are easily recognized since the locking bolt and its leaf spring were on opposite sides from the later Pattern 1879 Artillery Bayonet. These bayonets were designed to accompany the Mark I Artillery Carbine.

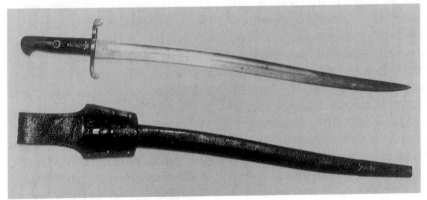

Diced leather grips were a feature of this Martini-Henry sword bayonet, shown here with its leather scabbard and frog.

61

Length overall: 31.2 inches
Blade length   25.8 inches

Pattern 1879 Artillery Bayonet

This is the standard production model of the bayonet noted. It has the button for the latch located on the right side of the pommel and the catch leaf spring on the left. The scabbard is iron mounted. These bayonets were new production and were designed to accompany the Mark I Artillery Carbine. The Pattern 1879 bayonets were officially classified as the Bayonet, Sword, B.L., Martini-Henry, Interchangeable, Artillery (Mark 1.).

Length overall 29.8 inches
Blade length: 24.3 inches

Bushed Yataghan Sword Bayonet

This bayonet was produced by bushing the muzzle ring of Yataghan-bladed bayonets intended for use on muzzleloading or Snider arms. It was produced for fitting to the Mark III Martini-Henry Artillery Carbine. Scabbards were iron mounted. A similar pattern of bayonet had been proposed for the Garrison Artillery Carbine.
Length overall: 28.1 inches
Blade length: 22.7 inches

Pattern 1887 Sword Bayonet

This bayonet was produced in four patterns that differ in blade design and locking bolt details. These bayonets were based on the bayonet developed for the .401-inch Enfield-Martini rifle and were used primarily with the Martini-Henry Mark IV rifles.
Scabbards were originally iron mounted, but a later pattern was brass mounted.

Pattern 1887 Mark I

This pattern was converted from the Enfield-Martini Second Pattern Model 1886 bayonet. It will be found with E-M markings on it. The blade had a single fuller, the locking latch had a leaf spring on the left side, and the checkered leather grips were held in place by four rivets.

Length overall: 23.75 inches
Blade length: 18.50 inches

Pattern 1887 Mark II

This bayonet was identical to the Mark I bayonet with one exception — the locking latch had a coil spring rather than the leaf spring of the Mark I. They were of new production. The checkered leather grips were held by two steel rivets.

Length overall: 23.75 inches
Blade length: 18.50 inches

Pattern 1887 Mark III

The blade on this model had no fuller, and a coil locking latch spring like the Mark II. Two rivets held the checkered leather grips.

Length overall: 23.75 inches
Blade length: 18.50 inches

Pattern 1887 Mark IV

These bayonets were converted from First Pattern Model 1886 Enfield-Martini Bayonets. The conversion was similar to the Mark I; however, the blade was lighter and the muzzle ring was closer to the blade.

Length overall: 23.75 inches
Blade length: 18.50 inches

Martini-Henry Rifle Specifications

Martini-Henry Rifle Mark I

Weight:
  Short butt: 8 lbs. 10 oz.
  Long butt: 8 lbs. 12 oz.

Length overall:
  Short butt: 49 inches
  Long butt: 49-1/2 inches

Barrel length:33.22 inches

Caliber: .450

Rifling: 7 grooves right hand twist, 1 in 22 inches.

Date of adoption:
  First pattern: June 1871
  Second pattern:
          3 September 1872
  Third pattern: 17 July 1874

Manufacturers: Royal Small Arms Factory, Enfield; Bir mingham Small Arms and Metal Company Ltd.; Lon don Small Arms Company Ltd.

Martini-Henry Rifle Mark II

Weight:
  Short butt: 8 lbs. 8 oz.
  Long butt: 8 lbs. 10 oz.

Length overall:
  Short butt: 49 inches
  Long butt: 49-1/2 inches

Barrel length:33.22 inches

Caliber: .450

Rifling: 7 grooves right twist, 1 in 22 inches.

Date of adoption:
          25 April 1877

Manufacturers: Royal Small Arms Factory, Enfield; Birmingham Small Arms and Metal Co. Ltd.; London Small Arms Co. Ltd.; Na tional Arms and Ammuni tion Co. Ltd.

Martini-Henry Rifle Mark III

Weight:
 Short butt: 8 lbs. 13-1/2oz.
 Long butt: 9 lbs. 1 oz.

Length overall:
 Short butt: 49.185 inches
 Long butt: 49.685 inches

Barrel length:33.187 inches

Caliber: .450

Rifling: 7 grooves right twist, 1 in 22 inches.

Date of adoption:
 22 August 1879

Manufacturers: Royal Small Arms Factory, Enfield; Birmingham Small Arms and Metal Co. Ltd.; London Small Arms Co. Ltd.; National Arms and Ammuni

Martini-Henry Rifle Mark IV (Type A, B, and C)

tion Co. Ltd.

Weight:
 Short butt: 9 lbs.
 Long butt: 9 lbs. 2 oz.

Length overall:
 (Type A and B)
 Short butt: 48.875 inches
 Long butt: 49.375 inches
 (Type C)
 Short butt: 49 inches
 Long butt: 49.5 inches

Barrel length:
 33.062 inches (Type A and B)
 33.187 inches (Type C)

Caliber: .450

Rifling: 7 grooves right hand twist, 1 in 22 inches

Date of Adoption:
 15 September 1887
 (all types)

Manufacturer: Royal Small Arms Factory, Enfield

Martini-Henry Carbine Specifications

Martini-Henry Carbine Mark I (Cavalry Carbine)

Weight: 7 lbs. 8 oz.

Length overall: 37.687 inches

Barrel length:21.375 inches

Caliber: .450

Rifling: 7 grooves right hand twist, 1 twist in 22 inches.

Date of Adoption:
            24 September 1877

Manufacturer: Royal Small Arms Factory, Enfield.

Martini-Henry Artillery Carbine Mark I

Weight: 7 lbs. 10-1/2 oz.

Length overall: 37.687 inches

Barrel length:21.375 inches

Caliber: .450

Rifling: 7 grooves right hand twist, 1 in 22 inches.

Date of Adoption:
            21 July 1879

Manufacturers: Royal Small Arms Factory, Enfield; Bir mingham Small Arms and Metal Co. Ltd.

Martini-Henry Garrison Artillery Carbine Mark I

Specifications as for Mark I Carbine (Cavalry)

Date of Adoption:
            9 April 1878

Manufacturer: Royal Small Arms Factory Enfield

Martini-Henry Artillery Carbine Mark II

Weight: 7 lbs. 9 oz.

Length overall: 37.687 inches

Barrel length:21.437 inches

Caliber: .450

Rifling: 7 grooves right hand twist, 1 in 22 inches

Date of Adoption:
                 18 August 1891

Manufacturer: Royal Small Arms Factory, Enfield (Conversion from Martini-Henry Rifle Mark II)

Martini-Henry Artillery Carbine Mark III

Weight: 7 lbs. 7 oz.

Length overall: 37.687 inches

Barrel length: 21.375 inches

Caliber: .450

Rifling: 7 grooves right hand twist, 1 turn in 22 inches.

Date of Adoption:
                 2 September 1891

Manufacturer: Royal Small Arms Factory, Enfield

Bibliography

1. *Catalog of the Enfield Pattern Room: British Rifles;* HMSO, London, 1981.

2. *Military Breech-Loading Rifles;* Majendie, V.D. and Browne, C.O., Royal Artillery Institution, Woolwich, 1870.

3. *American Breech Loading Small Arms;* Norton, C.B., F.W. Christern, NY, 1872.

4. *List of Changes In British War Material, Vol.I-IV;* Skennerton, I.D., Compiler, Skennerton, Margate, Australia, 1979-1993.

5. *A Treatise on the British Military Martini, Vol. I - III;* Temple, B.A. and Skennerton, I.D., Temple, Kilcoy, Australia, 1983-1995.

6. *Treatise on Military Small Arms and Ammunition,* 1888; HMSO, London, 1888.

7. *Regulations for Musketry Instruction,* 1887; HMSO, London, 1887.

8. *The Gun and Its Development,* 9th Edition; Greener, W.W., Greener, Birmingham, 1910.

9. *The Modern Shotgun, 2nd Edition;* Greener, W.W., Greener, Birmingham, 1891.

10. *Field Service Pocket Book* (various editions); HMSO, London.

Acknowledgments

The assistance of many people made this book possible. Al Petrillo not only edited this book, but also took all of the photographs shown in it. He also made every effort to keep the author at the keyboard.

My friend and fellow British military collector, Robert Washburn, gave great assistance and shared many items from his collection.

From Canada, assistance came from Andre Gousse, Yves Goyette, John Denner, and Mike Leclerc, who helped navigate the complicated Martini-Henry bayonet story.

In the United States, I must thank my brother, Fred Lewis, Don Fangboner, Tom Batha, and Bob Maze.

Other collectors and dealers in both Canada and the United States gave assistance over the years and are to numerous to mention. Never have I met a more helpful and pleasant group of people then those who have an interest in British arms.

Finally, I must thank my wife, Sharon, for her continued support and understanding of my researching and collecting British arms.

About the Author

Dennis Lewis lives in upstate New York with his wife, Sharon, and Webley, an English Springer Spaniel. His interest in British arms runs the full course, from the matchlock to the most current arms. He has a special interest in the period from the Crimean War to World War I.

He is well known in the field of American colonial history and the part that the Hudson-Champlain-Richelieu corridor has played in that story. He has taught at the college level, and written in that field for many years.

When not writing or teaching, he can be found building muzzleloading arms, engaging in eighteenth century re-enactments or out hunting with vintage British breechloading shotguns and his dog.